JARROLD SHORT WALKS

leisure walks for all ages

South London

Greenwich Millennium Village

Compiled by
Leigh Hatts

publishing

Mapping
sourced from Ordnance Survey®

Text: Leigh Hatts
Photography: Leigh Hatts
Editor: Donald Greig
Designer: Ellen Moorcraft

© Jarrold Publishing 2002

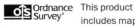 This product includes mapping data licensed from Ordnance Survey® with the permission of the Controller of Her Majesty's Stationery Office. © Crown Copyright 2002. All rights reserved. Licence number 100017593. Pathfinder is a registered trade mark of Ordnance Survey, the national mapping agency of Great Britain.

Jarrold Publishing ISBN 0-7117-2091-6

While every care has been taken to ensure the accuracy of the route directions, the publishers cannot accept responsibility for errors or omissions, or for changes in details given. The countryside is not static: hedges and fences can be removed, field boundaries can alter, footpaths can be rerouted and changes in ownership can result in the closure or diversion of some concessionary paths. Also, paths that are easy and pleasant for walking in fine conditions may become slippery, muddy and difficult in wet weather, while stepping-stones across rivers and streams may become impassable.

If you find an inaccuracy in either the text or maps, please write or e-mail Jarrold Publishing at one of the addresses below.

First published 2002
by Jarrold Publishing

Printed in Belgium
by Proost NV, Turnhout. 1/02

Jarrold Publishing
Pathfinder Guides, Whitefriars,
Norwich NR3 1TR
E-mail: pathfinder@jarrold.com
www.pathfinderguides.co.uk

Front cover: Tower Bridge from Rotherhithe
Previous page: Signpost to Greenwich Millennium Village

Contents

Keymap   4

Introduction   6

Walks

Short, easy walks

1   *Bermondsey Wall*   10
2   *Crystal Palace*   13
3   *Downe*   16
4   *Dulwich*   19
5   *Eltham Palace*   22
6   *Morden Hall*   25
7   *The Paris Garden*   28
8   *Shooters Hill*   31

Walks of modest length, likely to involve some modest uphill walking

9   *Beddington*   34
10 *The Dome*   37
11 *Greenwich*   40
12 *Wimbledon Common*   44
13 *Nonsuch*   47
14 *Ashtead and Epsom*   51
15 *Farnborough*   54
16 *Merstham*   57

More challenging walks which may be longer and/or over
more rugged terrain, often with some stiff climbs

17 *Addington*   61
18 *Coulsdon*   64
19 *Petts Wood*   68
20 *Richmond*   72

Further Information   76
Walking Safety; Follow the Country Code;
Useful Organisations; Ordnance Survey Maps
Answers to Questions   80

Keymap

SCALE 1:250 000 or 1 INCH to 4 MILES *1CM to 2.5KM*

```
0        2        4        6        8       10   KILOMETRES              15
0                2                4                6        MILES        8              10
```

KEYMAP HEIGHTS SHOWN IN FEET

Introduction

The routes and information in this book have been devised specifically with families and children in mind. All the walks include points of interest as well as a question to provide an objective.

If you, or your children, have not walked before, choose from the shorter walks for your first outings, although none of the walks is especially demanding. The purpose is not simply to get from A to B, but to enjoy an exploration, which may be just a steady stroll in the countryside.

The walks are graded by length and difficulty, but few landscapes are truly flat, especially those among the Chilterns. Even short walks may involve some ascent, but this is nowhere excessive. Details are given under Route Features in the first information box for each route. The precise nature of the ground underfoot, however, will depend on recent weather conditions. If you do set out on a walk and discover the going is harder than you expected, or the weather has deteriorated, do not be afraid to turn back. The route will always be there another day, when you are fitter or the children are more experienced or the weather is better.

London countryside

London has plenty of countryside within the M25 where 96 farms and at least 6,800 head of cattle can be found as well as ancient woodlands and commons.

Cows and sheep graze in Bromley and Richmond whilst horseriders can be seen setting out from stables in Mottingham, Chislehurst and even Croydon. Indeed cattle still roam the Thames-side Petersham meadows thanks to a recent arrangement which guarantees this pastoral scene for the future.

Herds of Royal deer run in Richmond Park, one of the largest walled urban parks, which continues to supply the traditional haunches of venison at Christmas for the tables of the Archbishop of Canterbury at Lambeth and the Lord Mayor in the City. The rural atmosphere has long

Eltham Palace bridge

been safeguarded and today the Royal Park is bringing in traffic calming measures to ensure that this old Surrey countryside trapped in the capital remains a living oasis. This, and other south London parks such as Beddington Park, are especially rewarding in autumn and spring when there are few visitors. Eltham Palace still offers the illusion of rolling countryside within sight of the City.

Use public transport

Although there is no need to go far to find countryside, London's public transport network is extensive and the service compares very favourably with other parts of the country. Such places as the National Trust's Petts Wood, Downe and Merstham on the Surrey borders can easily be reached from central London well within an hour.

Using public transport is strongly advised when setting out for a walk in London. Not only are London roads very crowded, with a notorious traffic jam record, but parking is very limited. Central London has been zoned for a congestion charge and many controlled parking zones have recently been introduced in London boroughs. Visitors to Southwark, for example, are advised not to arrive by car and the City across the river has implemented a severe traffic reduction policy. This does however increase the pleasure of exploring on foot.

Whilst many car parks at stations on the edge of London have pay and display car parks it should be noted that space is often limited on weekdays.

One Day or Weekend Travelcards, obtainable at Underground and mainline stations, are good value and allow all day travel on buses, Underground, rail and, in south London, also the new Tramlink. The ticket is especially useful when walking one of the linear routes along the Thames or between stations.

String of villages

It is often suggested that London is really a string of villages which have grown together. The sense of village is found even on a walk which begins at London Bridge. Its climax is the old dockland Rotherhithe village which retains its unique characteristics including Scandinavian churches founded to serve visiting sailors. Dulwich is in the Borough of Southwark, which includes Peckham and the Elephant & Castle, but Dulwich village is still a reality with a high street boasting a busy pub, post office, florist and food shop. The unique toll gate leads to a station which has a setting so wooded that its also a designated nature reserve.

Sampling long distance paths

This book offers the chance to sample many long distance routes. The central London walks include a section of the Thames Path national trail which links the capital with the Home Counties and beyond. The Dome walk enjoys the latest and probably least known section of the Thames Path. Occasionally on other routes it is possible to see the London Loop waymark indicating that the path is part of the 140 mile London Outer Orbital Path which circles inner London.

There is plenty to discover and inspire within London and these walks enjoyed at different times will reveal different seasons in all their splendour and allow for new experiences.

London's growth

At first, thanks to the Romans, London was just the City of London or what we today call the Square Mile where the City churches and financial institutions are found. The Tower of London on the east side was outside London – it is still outside the City – and Westminster to the west was a palace and a monastery on a triangular island created by the Thames on one side and the River Tyburn on the other two.

Holwood House near Keston

South of the Thames was not London but countryside later called Surrey. When Mary I prepared to return to London with her new husband, Philip of Spain, she went first to the country home of the Bishop of Winchester in Southwark. She went for a ride around the farmland before entering the capital by crossing London Bridge.

As late as 1689 William II was able to claim that he was moving to the country when he left Whitehall for Kensington Palace. Even in Queen Victoria's reign London was said to end at Hyde Park Corner where the Duke of Wellington lived. His house, being the first passed by a traveller arriving from the west, was known as 'Number One London', being the first house on the capital's edge.

By the end of Victoria's reign there had been dramatic growth. The Metropolitan Police and the London County Council had both been established to operate with wide boundaries. Eventually Middlesex was embraced and by 1965 the present County of London boundary had been established by eating into the other Home Counties. Now there are 32 large boroughs within the Greater London boundary. This circle is large enough to include many green spaces in Essex and Surrey saved by the Corporation of London which for over a century has pursued a policy of preserving outstanding countryside threatened with development.

These and other green lungs long enjoyed by Londoners are now officially within Greater London.

● Spectacular river views ● dark dockland streets

1 *Bermondsey Wall*

START	London Bridge
DISTANCE	2 miles (3.4km)
APPROXIMATE TIME	1½ hours
PARKING	None
ROUTE FEATURES	Riverside paths

This riverside walk provides a succession of memorable views of the Thames and the historic buildings overlooking the river.

Tower Bridge is seen from Cherry Garden Pier at its best framing St Paul's. A new footbridge over St Saviour's Dock means that the walker rarely has to divert from the Bermondsey waterside.

👞 On the south end of London Bridge go down the steps on the right hand side just behind the leaning arm at Southwark Tourist Centre. The wide steps lead down to the river. A plaque on the left indicates the original line of earlier London Bridges. Walk ahead to pass modern Cotton's Atrium and Hay's Galleria, a shopping arcade which was once a dock. HMS *Belfast* is permanently moored in the river here.

Ⓐ Pass City Hall to reach Potter's Field and continue under Tower Bridge. The cobbled road ahead is the cavernous Shad Thames. Go left into easily missed Maggie Blake's Cause to reach the Butler's Wharf riverfront. At the far end there is the Design Museum.

Ⓑ Cross the swing bridge at the mouth of St Saviour's Dock and follow the passage into Mill Street. At once go left to keep east along Bermondsey Wall West. At the end go right and

PUBLIC TRANSPORT Underground (Northern Line, Jubilee Line) or rail to London Bridge Station

REFRESHMENTS Cafés and pubs on the riverside

PUBLIC TOILETS Hay's Galleria

ORDNANCE SURVEY MAPS Explorer 173 (London North)

Christopher Jones memorial

left into Chambers Street to avoid Chambers Wharf. Take the first left, Loftie Street, and after the bend bear left at Fountain Green

Square to join the riverside path on Bermondsey Wall East. Opposite is Wapping. Pass the Dr Salter sculpture on a seat and Cherry Garden Pier.

C The way becomes a road passing between the Angel pub and the remains of Edward III's palace. Continue past a lonely house which was once part of a Thames-side terrace, to return to the riverside by a park. Soon the path becomes cloistered with a break for King's Stairs at

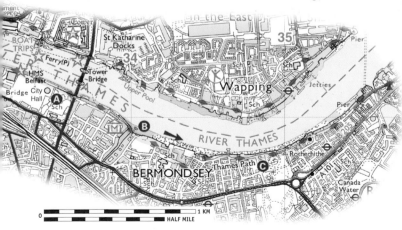

0 _____ 1 KM
HALF MILE

Tower Bridge from Bermondsey Wall

Rotherhithe. The path double bends to leave the river and enter narrow Rotherhithe Street. Pass between tall warehouses and St Mary's Church with its modern sculpture memorial to the *Mayflower's* Captain Christopher Jones.

The Pilgrim Fathers' *Mayflower* sailed to America in 1620 from the jetty behind Rotherhithe's **Mayflower** pub. Her captain, Christopher Jones, is commemorated at St Mary's Church. Buried outside is Prince Lee Boo who sailed here in 1780 from the Pelau Islands. Being a dockland village there are also Finnish and Norwegian churches built for visiting sailors and now serving a scattered Scandinavian community. The public toilets at the end of Albion Street have Men and Women signs in Norwegian.

To visit the church follow the road to the right round the churchyard. The main walk continues ahead at the junction by the Mayflower pub. Continue forward along the now wider Rotherhithe Street to the second open wharf on the left.

Turn left on to Cumberland Wharf only to see the sculpture of the child reading Sunshine Weekly. But the walk continues to the right down Swan Road. At the main road go right to reach Rotherhithe station and Rotherhithe Station. ●

? *What is lurking on the river wall near Cherry Garden Pier?*

Crystal Palace

START	Crystal Palace
DISTANCE	2 miles (3.4km)
APPROXIMATE TIME	2 hours
PARKING	Paddock Car park near station
ROUTE FEATURES	Park paths

2

Crystal Palace is both a landmark and a viewpoint with gardens, including Britain's largest fern garden, lakes, islands, a maze, a cricket ground and 25 prehistoric monsters. Until Wembley Stadium opened in 1924 the FA Cup Final was played here. This is also home to the National Sports Centre.

At the station entrance go right. Go up the steps and on entering the park turn left to a road junction. Turn right to go through the Canada Gates alongside the National Sports Centre entrance. Follow the path, which may have some traffic at first. Over to the left is the wall of the Crystal Palace terrace.

A On reaching the main junction turn left to go up the central Palace steps. At the top turn round for a panoramic view as far as the Surrey Hills.

Turn right, with the steps to the right, to walk to the far end of the site. Over to the left is the tall TV transmitter. On entering the main park follow the path ahead which curves down to the right to join a main path in front of the concert bowl. Stay on the wide path, a former racetrack, as it curves

The park takes its name from the glass exhibition hall which was brought here from Hyde Park after the **Great Exhibition** of 1851. It was designed by Joseph Paxton whose large bust is now in front of the main entrance. The huge greenhouse was made of 4,000 tons of iron and 400 tons of glass with 30 miles of complicated guttering. Here it was the park's central feature until destroyed by a fire, seen from all over London, in 1936.

PUBLIC TRANSPORT Rail to Crystal Palace Station from London Bridge or Victoria Station
REFRESHMENTS Park café
PUBLIC TOILETS Opposite café
CHILDREN'S PLAY AREA In Jubilee Park, by the car park
ORDNANCE SURVEY MAPS Explorer 161 (London South)

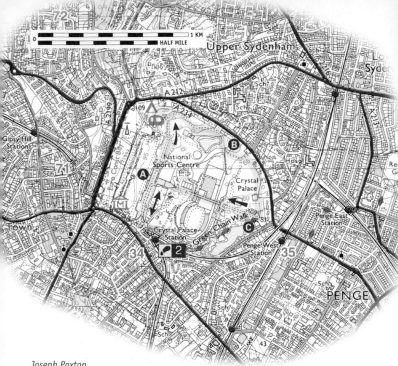

Joseph Paxton

round to the right. Soon there is a view through trees down on to the lake.

B Just after a path joins from the right go left. Keep forward at another junction to go round the far side of a cricket field. On the way there is the One O'clock Club and a first aid post. Beyond a small car park there is the main park path **C**.

Sphinx at Crystal Palace

Turn right up the main avenue passing between the information centre and the café. At the far end go left only to view the monsters.

The 29 prehistoric monsters were made in 1854 creating the world's first prehistoric animal park. They are constructed with brick and iron covered in painted stucco and were made by **Waterhouse Hawkins** whose expert advisor did not have the advantage of 21st-century 'Jurassic' research. Among the outstanding animals is an Irish Elk which has undergone painstaking restoration. The creatures now stand with an authentic backdrop of prehistoric flora and fauna.

The main walk continues up steps on the right. Turn sharp left to find more steps on the right. At the top of this flight continue ahead on a high walkway running through the National Sports Centre. At the end go through a gateway to find a huge bust of Joseph Paxton.

Continue forward and, before the steps, turn left to return to Crystal Palace Station. ●

What is the large black marble gorilla behind the café called?

3 Downe

START Downe

DISTANCE 2 miles (3.4km)

APPROXIMATE TIME 1½ hours

PARKING Roadside parking in village

ROUTE FEATURES Footpaths may be muddy

Downe is best known for naturalist Charles Darwin's house which still retains the old spelling of Down. The 'e' was added to the village name in the 19th century to avoid confusion with County Down in Ireland. 'It is surprising to think London is only 16 miles off' observed Darwin and this is still true today.

From the village square walk up Luxted Road. When the pavement on the left ends cross the road to a gate and follow the enclosed footpath. Beyond a stile bear left up a long field to a gate on the right. Cross the centre of the next field to a stile in the corner. After a second stile the way is gently downhill to a path junction.

A Turn left through a tunnel of trees to reach steep West Hill. Cross the road to continue along the wooded valley side. Where a sign points to Downe turn left to go up steps to a stile. Go forward and then bear half left across the field to the far corner.

In Downe village

PUBLIC TRANSPORT Bus from Bromley South Station

REFRESHMENTS Pubs and café at Down House

PUBLIC TOILETS None

ORDNANCE SURVEY MAPS Explorer 147 (Sevenoaks & Tonbridge)

Downe Church is over 700 years old but has a window marking Robin Knox-Johnson's 20th-century round-the-world voyage. There is also plaque to John Lubbock who invented bank holidays. Outside on the tower is the Darwin memorial sundial. Elizabeth I witnessed a christening here in 1559 just after becoming Queen.

Cross a stile and at once go right through a gate on to Darwin's Sandwalk. To the left is the Down House walled kitchen garden.

(You may walk through the garden to buy a visitor's ticket or visit the café.) Continue through the kissing gate ahead. Bear half right across the field. At a gate go over the stile and cross a road to a gap in the hedge opposite.

B A path runs ahead over a field. On the far side, at a junction of paths, turn left along the side of the same field and turn left again at the field corner. The boundary on the right ends at a lonely kissing gate. Go through the gate and over

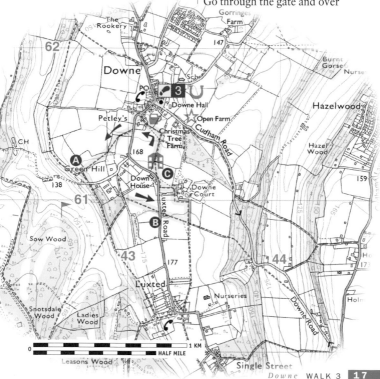

Downe village centre

concrete paths to pass in front of Downe Court farmhouse. Keep forward through a gap and over grass to a stile. Turn left to walk over a hard surface to a stile. Once in the field keep ahead and on the far side bear right to reach a stile on the left leading to the road. Down House is opposite.

C Do not cross the stile but bear half right across to the far corner where there is a kissing gate behind the holly. In the next field keep forward. Christmas Tree Farm can

Charles Darwin and his large family lived at Down House from 1842 until his death here in 1882. His chair and desk remain in the ground floor study where he produced his famous book *The Origin of Species*. The restored walled kitchen garden again has strawberries, different potatoes, peas, beans, cabbages and gooseberries. **The Sandwalk** was Darwin's 'thinking path' where the great scientist walked every morning in deep thought.

be seen ahead. At the corner turn left over a stile into another field. Go right and at the second corner keep ahead down a passage to emerge between houses in Luxted Road. Turn right to reach Downe village square. ●

? *Who is the Queen on the Queen's Head pub sign?*

Dulwich

START Dulwich
DISTANCE 2 miles (3.4km)
APPROXIMATE TIME 1½ hours
PARKING Sydenham Hill Station (pay and display)
ROUTE FEATURES Steep hill and woodland paths which may be muddy

Dulwich is so rural that even the station is a nature reserve managed by the London Wildlife Trust which also cares for some nearby woodland. This walk is on the fringes of Dulwich where there is a toll gate, open space and hillside woods. On the hilltop there is an Italianate villa which has become a pub.

Turn left out of Sydenham Hill Station forecourt to walk down College Road. Ahead is the Dulwich toll gate.

A Beyond the gate and lodge turn right into Grange Lane. Follow the road, which carries mainly traffic for the golf club, as it bends to the right and climbs past allotments. At the top there is the Dulwich and Sydenham Hill Golf Club and the South London Scout Centre. Keep going ahead as the way

Dulwich Wood House pub

PUBLIC TRANSPORT Rail to Sydenham Hill Station from Victoria Station
REFRESHMENTS Dulwich Wood House pub at top of hill
PUBLIC TOILETS None
ORDNANCE SURVEY MAPS Explorer 161 (London South)

narrows and at once turn right to enter Dulwich Wood at a kissing gate.

B The woodland path gently rises to reach a clearing and a five-way junction. Take the second path on the left. This runs alongside a fence to the right. The narrow way runs through more woodland. At a divide bear right across a crosspath. Soon there is a felled tree trunk, with a handy step, to cross just before the path reaches Sydenham Hill Wood.

> **?** *Why is there a stone and post on the corner of Crescent Wood Road and Sydenham Hill?*

The Dulwich village **toll gate** was set up in 1789 when the road was made up for cattle using grazing land owned by the nearby Dulwich College. The board still lists the charges for 'sheep, lambs or hogs per score' as well as 6d for 'every Motor Car, Motor Cycle or Motor Cycle Combination'. Pedestrians can pass through free of charge. Most other London toll gates were abolished in 1864.

Later the way crosses another path before rising alongside the now blocked railway tunnel. The stepped path bends to pass across the top of the tunnel entrance. At a T-junction bear right up to a kissing gate leading to Crescent Wood Road.

Dulwich toll gate

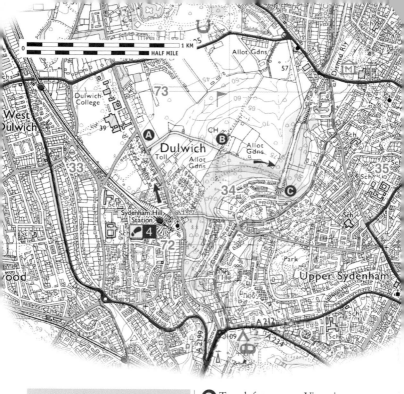

Charles I hunted in **Dulwich Woods** where local people had to 'forebeare to hunt, chase, molest or hurt the king's stagges'. A century later it was used by smugglers and was also home to gypsies. Dulwich and adjoining Sydenham Hill Woods are the largest remaining tract of the old Great North Wood which stretched from Deptford to Selhurst.

Sydenham Hill Wood is now a unique mix of old and recent woodland and is home to over 200 species of trees and flowering plants including wild garlic. Birds that are found here include the woodpecker.

C Turn left to pass a Victorian post box. At the main road go right along Sydenham Hill to find the far end of Crescent Wood Road by Dulwich Wood House pub. Here go right and after a short distance turn left through the white kissing gate into Low Cross Wood Lane. The wide way runs steeply downhill through Dulwich Wood. At the bottom, where there is a view of the spire of St Stephen's Church, go through another kissing gate and cross the road to Sydenham Hill station opposite. ●

5 *Eltham Palace*

START Mottingham
DISTANCE 2 miles (3.4km)
APPROXIMATE TIME 1½ hours
PARKING Roadside parking in Middle Park Avenue by station
ROUTE FEATURES Gentle climb and path which may be muddy

This route cuts across a strip of remaining countryside on the edge of Eltham where a former royal residence survives. There are striking views of the capital indicating that this retreat was within easy reach of both London and the palace at Greenwich. Today's landmarks include the London Eye, the BT Tower, St Paul's Cathedral and Canary Wharf.

From Mottingham Station walk up the approach road to the main road and turn left. Go left again into Middle Park Avenue.

A Where the wide grass verge on the right ends, opposite Shrubshall Close, go right through a kissing gate. A winding footpath gently rises. On reaching a field keep forward with Eltham Palace visible to the right.

B At the far end a kissing gate leads to King John's Walk and a view across London. Go right and soon the view opens out to the left. Beyond a gate there are stables. At a junction go right up a rising path to the main entrance to Eltham Palace where a bridge spans the moat.

Turn left to walk away from the bridge with the timber-framed Lord Chancellor's Lodgings to the left. At a junction go sharp right

> **Eltham Palace** was a royal country home where Henry VIII enjoyed spending Christmas at the moated building. Cardinal Wolsey also stayed here. Geoffrey Chaucer had been in charge of early modest building work but in 1479 the great hall with its hammerbeam roof was added. The adjacent Thirties-style house, built on by the Courtauld family, adds contrast.

PUBLIC TRANSPORT Rail to Mottingham Station from Charing Cross Station
REFRESHMENTS Shops near station
PUBLIC TOILETS The Tarn park
ORDNANCE SURVEY MAPS Explorer 162 (Greenwich & Gravesend)

past The Gatehouse to enter Tiltyard Approach. Pass the gateway to The Tiltyard and follow the long high brick wall.

C At the crossroads go right along Court Road. Here there are several interesting Victorian houses. Soon on the right is the entrance to the Royal Blackheath Golf Club which occupies Eltham

? *What is the brick structure just inside the gate at The Tarn?*

Lodge. Continue along the road to The Tarn park on the left.

Go through The Tarn's first gate and down the steps. Turn sharp right to the end of the lake. Here go left to follow the water and

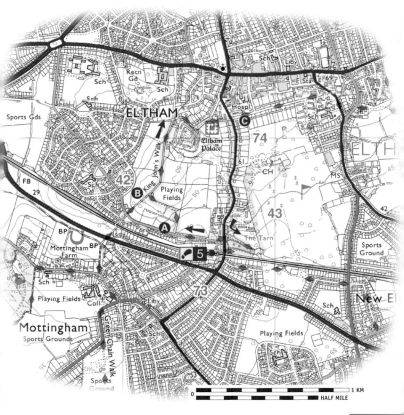

The Tarn, which includes a bird sanctuary, was once part of the grounds of Eltham Palace and later nearby Eltham Lodge, built in 1664 as a more comfortable successor to the large palace. Then water here was known as Starbucks Pond and Mottingham villagers used to skate on it when the surface froze during cold winters.

cross the bridge at the opposite end. Once on the far bank go right and at a fork bear left to rejoin the road. Opposite is Mottingham Station.

Morden Hall

6

START Morden
DISTANCE 2 miles (3.4km)
APPROXIMATE TIME 2 hours
PARKING Car park in
Morden Hall Road
ROUTE FEATURES
Meadowland

Morden Hall Park is a remarkable slice of countryside trapped in south London. The meadows (free) are open from dawn to dusk as is the farm. The old estate buildings are occupied by the National Trust shop and café and other rooms can also be visited. The kitchen garden is now a garden centre. A tramway runs through the park.

At Morden Station forecourt use the crossing to walk over to the far side of London Road and go ahead into Aberconway Road.

A At the far end cross Morden Hall Road to enter the Morden Hall Park gateway. Go past the main National Trust buildings to the right and later the stables on the left.

On reaching the Snuff Mill do not cross the river but bear left to follow the water. Pass through a gateway, with a view of Morden Hall to the left, to a second bridge where a signpost points to the Tramway. Turn right to cross the bridge and walk up the avenue

ahead. The path bends and where it turns sharply go left onto a rough path cutting across the meadow.

Morden Hall stables

PUBLIC TRANSPORT Underground to Morden Station (Northern Line)
REFRESHMENTS National Trust Riverside Café
PUBLIC TOILETS At the National Trust tearoom and farm
ORDNANCE SURVEY MAPS Explorer 161 (London South)

The moated **Morden Hall** was built around 1750 by the Hatfield family who ran the snuff mill. The parkland passed to the National Trust in 1941. The meadow hay is cut once a year. The River Wandle flows through the park in man-made channels with islands left inaccessible so that wildlife can live without disturbance. There is also a rose garden. The big house is now a restaurant.

? *Where does the River Wandle rise and end?*

B At the far side go through a gate and turn left to cross the Tramway level crossing at Phipps Bridge Tram Stop. Go ahead down a passage and turn left into Phipps Bridge Road. Later, on the left, there is the 18th-century Wandle

Villa and just beyond is the castellated Lodge. Continue along the road to pass Everett's Place cottages and reach a junction with Haslemere Avenue.

Morden Hall park

C Turn left to cross Phipps Bridge, a Bailey bridge structure. Ahead is Dean City Farm. The walk continues to the left through a gap into Bunce's Meadow which is part of Morden Hall Park. A straight path runs parallel to the river on the left before bearing round to the right. Cross a stream and turn left to go over the tram line.

On the far side of the track the path is fenced. At a junction go left to follow a winding path across the wetland and meadows. White and yellow wild flowers bloom here in summer. Cross three bridges, ignoring a turning to the right, to follow the path in front of Morden Hall, past the bridge crossed earlier and back to the snuff mill and main National Trust buildings. Go ahead at the main gates up Aberconway Road to reach Morden Station and the starting point of the walk. ●

7

The Paris Garden

START Southwark Station
DISTANCE 2 miles (3.4km)
APPROXIMATE TIME 1 hour
PARKING None
ROUTE FEATURES Riverside path and pavements

The now lost Paris Garden, between today's Oxo Tower and Tate Modern, was one of several riverside estates facing the City of London. Although much of the ground has now been built over the mysterious name lives on in a street sign and there are small fragments of garden trapped between buildings.

🖊 Turn right out of Southwark Station to walk along The Cut. Go right along Hatfields.

Hopton's Almshouses and Tate Modern

At the second crossroads, Stamford Street, go ahead over the crossing to turn left.

A After crossing the end of Broadwall go ahead into Bernie Spain Gardens and bear right. At the far end go through the gateway and cross Upper Ground to enter the park opposite. Follow the path to the riverside.

Go right to walk downstream in front of Oxo Tower Wharf. Keep by the river to pass under Blackfriars Bridge and the railway bridge to reach Bankside. Ahead is the Founders Arms.

Behind the pub turn inland down

PUBLIC TRANSPORT Underground to Southwark Station (Jubilee Line)
REFRESHMENTS Cafés in The Cut and on the riverside
PUBLIC TOILETS On Bankside
ORDNANCE SURVEY MAPS Explorer 173 (London North)

? *Why are there empty pillars in the river between the two bridges?*

The **Paris Garden** was the medieval riverside estate next to the Bishop of Winchester's parkland to the east and the Duchy of Cornwall marshes to the west. The name probably comes from the word parish. The street called Broadwall marks the boundary with the marshes and Boundary Row speaks for itself. There was a moated manor house and William Shakespeare visited its Swan Theatre.

steps and through the archway by the shops. Bear half right to walk past the Furniture Union shop and up Hopton Street. On the left is Nell Gwynne's House and Hopton's Almshouses.

B At Southwark Street continue ahead down Bear Lane to the White Hart. Go left to the pub and at once right into Great Suffolk Street to go under a bridge. At the junction by the Union Jack go right under another bridge and left by the Lord Nelson into Nelson

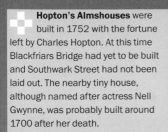

Hopton's Almshouses were built in 1752 with the fortune left by Charles Hopton. At this time Blackfriars Bridge had yet to be built and Southwark Street had not been laid out. The nearby tiny house, although named after actress Nell Gwynne, was probably built around 1700 after her death.

G Turn right along Surrey Row. At Blackfriars Road go ahead into Boundary Row opposite. At Ufford Street go left to pass some Church Commissioners' cottages but soon go right into Short Street which leads to The Cut. Opposite is the Young Vic Theatre.

Square. Ahead is a plaque to the poet Shelley. Keep forward towards the old houses and at the corner The Oxo Tower keep ahead down the side.

Turn right along The Cut. On the way cross the pedestrian crossing to be on the left-hand side for Southwark Station and the staring point of the walk.

Shooters Hill

8

START The Bull pub at top of Shooters Hill

DISTANCE 2 miles (3.4km)

APPROXIMATE TIME 1½ hours

PARKING Crown Woods Lane off Kenilworth Gardens

ROUTE FEATURES Grass, woodland and pavements

The milestone outside Shooters Hill church reads '8 miles to London Bridge'. This 133- metre high hill, visible from central London's Millennium Bridge, gave travellers from abroad their first view of the capital as they came over the brow on the Roman Watling Street. Half the hill remains as natural woodland.

Walk along the main road from the Bull towards the landmark water tower. Below the tower go left into Cleanthus Road. The roadway bears to the right and then to the left. When the line of houses on the right ends go right up steps to a playground on the hill's highest point. Ahead is a view over Kent to a ridge of hills. Go ahead over the grass down to the road below.

A Turn left along Eaglesfield Road to pass the end of Foxcroft Road on the left. Pass a tennis

Shooters Hill water tower

PUBLIC TRANSPORT Bus to Shooters Hill

REFRESHMENTS The Bull pub on hilltop

PUBLIC TOILETS None

ORDNANCE SURVEY MAPS Explorer 162 (Greenwich & Gravesend)

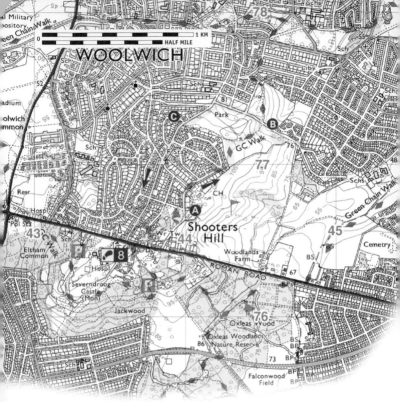

Shooters Hill was on the pilgrim route to Canterbury and the main Dover road. Samuel Pepys wrote about the hill and Charles Dickens describes the mail coach passing here in *A Tale of Two Cities*. Earlier the woods had been the haunt of highwaymen. The summit, once a place for executions, now has the landmark water tower built in 1910. The **Bull pub** is the successor to one recorded in 1687 by Daniel Defoe. A surprise among the houses is a burial mound suggesting a Pre-Roman settlement on this strategic site.

club with views and continue ahead as the way becomes Kinlet Road. At the junction with Mereworth Drive and Ashridge Crescent go right to find a footpath on the left running along the side of number 63.

On entering Shrewsbury Park go ahead over the grass, with houses over to the left, to reach a metalled path. Turn right and follow the path which runs downhill giving views towards Dartford.

B At the bottom of the hill go left to follow a rough path uphill. At the top go ahead over grass keeping parallel to a road down to right. Beyond are more views of the Thames. The ground rises to meet Plum Lane.

Turn left uphill but keep inside the high fence. Where the rough path divides in the woodland keep near the fence to enjoy the views down on to the Dome.

? *What are the white steps for at the top of Shooters Hill?*

C At the far end continue ahead along Plum Lane. By tiny Mayplace

Eaglesfield, the hill's highest point, is named after eagles on the shield of an 18th-century High Sheriff of Kent, whose county can be seen from here as well as Essex and London. This was once part of a garden and nearby Shrewsbury Lane recalls the original Shrewsbury House, where in 1799 three year old Princess Charlotte, daughter of the Prince Regent, was sent to live quietly away from the excitements of her father's Carlton House off The Mall.

Lane on the right there is an ancient burial mound. Here the road becomes Shrewsbury Lane. Keep straight on. Later there are more spectacular views on the right down Occupation Lane and Ankerdine Crescent. Continue ahead, back to the Bull. ●

View over Woolwich from Shrewsbury Park

9 *Beddington*

START Hackbridge
DISTANCE 3½ miles (5.6km)
APPROXIMATE TIME 1½ hours
PARKING Hackbridge Station (pay and display)
ROUTE FEATURES Park and new plantation paths which can both be muddy

Beddington Park is a rare example of stately home parkland which, having previously contracted, is in the 21st century expanding. A waterworks built over part of the estate has been partly reopened and replanted attracting birds and wildlife. A new path provides the perfect access from a handy station to the main parkland, which includes the site of a lost village.

Turn right out of the Hackbridge Station forecourt to walk along London Road. At a junction go right into the now very short Mile Road. Pass through the kissing gate ahead and follow the narrow path as it rises to cross the railway. Ahead can be seen church spires in Broad Green. On the far side, at the bottom of the slope, turn right on a gravel path running through the Beddington's former waterworks now planted with young trees.

A The way bends and beyond a kissing gate enters Beddington Park. Go right but before the

gateway turn left on to a path running across grass and into the

Beddington Church

PUBLIC TRANSPORT Rail to Hackbridge Station
REFRESHMENTS Café in Beddington Park
PUBLIC TOILETS Alongside park café
ORDNANCE SURVEY MAPS Explorers 161 (London South)

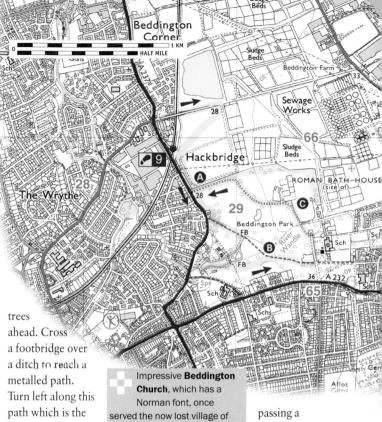

trees ahead. Cross a footbridge over a ditch to reach a metalled path. Turn left along this path which is the former carriageway to the manor house. Just before the bridge at the River Wandle turn right to follow the river and the side of the lake.

The river runs into the lake in front of The Grange. Stay by the water

Impressive **Beddington Church**, which has a Norman font, once served the now lost village of Beddington. The next door **Carew Manor** has a hall with a 15th-century hammerbeam roof. Henry VIII visited Sir Nicholas Carew here but eight years later had him executed for alleged treason. In the following century oranges were grown in the garden. The Carew family stayed until 1859 and the mansion is now a school. Nearby half-timbered and elaborate East Lodge was designed by a church architect 'Joseph Clarke' in 1887.

passing a footbridge spanning the lake. The path goes through a gate, narrows and crosses a tiny footbridge spanning a channel. At the far end cross a waterfall and bear round to the left to walk along the opposite bank. On reaching the footbridge again turn right into a long avenue but after a few yards go left along another avenue.

B At a junction bear right on a path which soon runs along the side of a walled burial ground with the church seen ahead. Go left at Church Road to pass between the burial ground entrance to the left and both the church and Carew Manor on the right. At East Lodge ahead bear left. Cross the River Wandle and keep forward. There is a cricket field to the right.

C At the bend there is Parkside Café and a children's playground. The path curves again to run alongside the Park's northern boundary. Just before the gateway

The Grange is a rebuild of an 1860s house destroyed by fire in 1960. The garden with the topiary and stone bridge survived. Its lake is a former mill pond for a now demolished mill which produced paper and flour from the 1770s.

to the road ahead go right to the hidden kissing gate and path leading from Beddington Park into the former waterworks.

At a junction go left up the sloping path running across Mile Road Bridge and down to London Road. Turn left for Hackbridge Station. ●

? *What is the high eight-sided building to the north of Carew Manor?*

Topiary hedge at The Grange

The Dome

START North Greenwich Station
DISTANCE 3½ miles (5.6km)
TIME 1½ hours
PARKING Dome car park (pay and display)
ROUTE FEATURES New and rough riverside paths

A new riverside path by the Dome and across Victoria Deep Water Terminal allows exploration of Blackwall Point for the first time in over a century. It also creates a contrast between a new promenade and a working dockside. There are spectacular views of the Thames Barrier and the confluence of the Rivers Thames and Lea as seen from the air on Eastenders.

At the underground exit go left along the glass bus station. Go through the last door and bear left

Giant sculpture

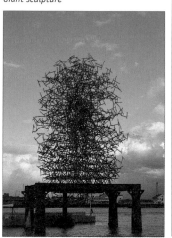

to follow the road round to the right passing two more bus stops. At the junction with Edmund Halley Way go left and then turn right along West Parkside. Walk on the left hand side when following this new Dome approach road.

A Turn left at River Way to pass the Pilot pub. At the far end of the wide cobbled street go left up steps to East Parkside. Turn left along the road and then right on a path running to the river.

B Turn right on the riverside path only to view the Millennium Village **C** from the riverside path. The main walk continues to the left

PUBLIC TRANSPORT Underground to North Greenwich Station
REFRESHMENTS The Pilot in River Way
PUBLIC TOILETS By route at Limpley Stoke
ORDNANCE SURVEY MAPS Explorer 162 (Greenwich & Gravesend)

River Way is a rare old street dating from the time when this was known as East Greenwich rather than North. The Pilot pub, opened in 1801, is alongside the Ceylon Place cottages. Before the Millennium its customers were gas workers and people who moored boats on London's last natural beach. Now the future drinkers will most likely come from the Millennium Village behind and Thames Path walkers who set out from, or arrive at, the Thames Barrier starting point.

passes the Dome Pier and the Dome's main entrance over to the left. Later there is Richard Wilson's Slice of Reality sculpture which gives the impression of a moored ship.

D As the riverside path turns south-west there is a sculptured milepost just before lines, on each side of the path, marking the

> **?** At the River Lea entrance there is a lonely church to the right. What is the tall round building on the left?

on the Thames Path which runs round the northern tip of Blackwall Point. On the way it

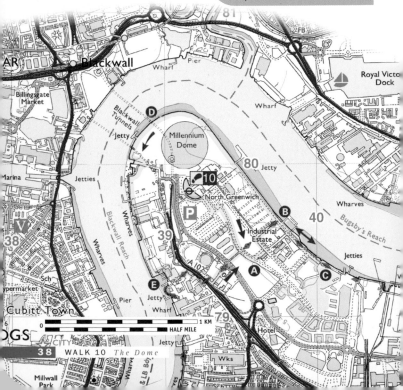

Greenwich Meridian. On the west side the way is briefly inland to cross the end of Drawdock Road. Continue near the river to pass over Delta Wharf. At a path junction do not go right to Tunnel Avenue but keep ahead to cross Victoria Deep Water Terminal where gravel is landed.

E At the far end the path goes inland and right along the back of a building. At a T-junction turn left down a path to reach the main road leading to Blackwall Tunnel.

The Millennium Dome

The **Dome** was built as the focus for the UK's Millennium celebrations and housed the controversial year-long exhibition. The structure, designed by Richard Rogers, is not only the world's largest dome but also has the largest roof in the world. The site is former marshland which for over a century was a vast gasworks. Below the Dome is North Greenwich Station opened in 1999 for the 2000 exhibition but also serving the nearby 1,400-home Millennium Village built to environmentally friendly standards.

Ahead is the peninsula's last gas holder. Turn right and after a short distance cross the road by going over the high footbridge.

Once on the far side go left past a post box and left down Boord Street to pass a redundant weighbridge. Cross Millennium Way and follow the path ahead. At West Parkside go left to follow the road to the Dome and North Greenwich Station.

11 *Greenwich*

START Blackheath Station
DISTANCE 3½ miles (5.6km)
APPROXIMATE TIME 2½ hours
PARKING Blackheath Grove opposite station (pay & display)
ROUTE FEATURES Grass, steep hills and views

The vast open space of Blackheath has hosted many historic events and today it is the starting point for the annual London Marathon. Down below is Greenwich which for a time was the centre of government and naval defence. The viewpoint panorama of the famous Greenwich buildings contrasts with the growing cluster of Canary Wharf skyscrapers opposite.

Pond at Blackheath

From Blackheath Station turn left and at the fork cross the road to go uphill on the left hand side.

At a crossroads bear left with Montpelier Vale and cross the main road into All Saints Drive.

PUBLIC TRANSPORT Rail to Blackheath
REFRESHMENTS Pubs and cafés in Greenwich
PUBLIC TOILETS In Greenwich Park and near Cutty Sark
ORDNANCE SURVEY MAPS Explorer 162 (Greenwich & Gravesend)

Keep the church to
the right and walk ahead on the
path. Bear right at Talbot Place
where it forks and head towards
the landmark towers of Canary
Wharf in the distance. The way
crosses Long Pond Road and a

In Greenwich Park a new
oak tree has been planted
alongside the ancient
Queen Elizabeth's oak by
Baron Greenwich. What
is his better known name?

main road before running up to the Greenwich Park gates.

A Continue ahead down the avenue of horse chestnuts to the viewpoint at the far end by General Wolfe's massive statue. From here there is a panorama of Docklands and London from St Paul's Cathedral to the Dome with Greenwich below.

B Bear left to pass the Royal Observatory building and go through a kissing gate to cross the Greenwich Meridian marked on the ground. Turn left at a junction and where the path meets the wide park drive turn right to continue

Henry VIII was born at **Greenwich Palace** and married Catherine of Aragon here. Sir Christopher Wren's replacement buildings, for many years housing the Royal Naval College, are now occupied by the University of Greenwich. The National Maritime Museum includes The Queen's House designed by Inigo Jones for James I's wife and built to span the line of the old main road. St Alphege's stands on the site of Archbishop Alphege's martyrdom by invading Danes in 1012. Those buried inside include composer Thomas Tallis and General Wolfe. The Cutty Sark tea clipper has been in dry dock since 1954.

downhill to St Mary's Gate. Go ahead down King William Walk,

Houses at Blackheath

over the main road using the crossing to the right, to reach the Cutty Sark in its dry dock.

Before the river go right through a gateway into the grounds of the former Royal Naval College. Stay on the path ahead which soon runs close to the river, with views of the Isle of Dogs, and past the main buildings. Often music is heard coming from Trinity College of Music. At the far end, opposite the Trafalgar Tavern, bear right to find lodges and a gateway on the left.

C Go through the gates and turn right up Park Row. At the main road the crossing is to the right. Continue ahead to enter Greenwich Park. A children's

boating lake and playground are to the left.

Keep forward as a gentle climb begins. Bear slightly left at a crossways on to the broadest of the paths which continues to climb. At the top go right at a T-junction and then take the first path to the left. The entrance to the flower gardens is to the right. Leave the Park by the gateway and turn right.

D At the road junction keep ahead with the monument to the right. At Shooter's Hill Road cross on the crossing and take the path ahead across the grass. Cross a second road to a pond and turn right. Follow the road past the Prince of Wales pub and downhill to Blackheath Station. ●

Blackheath may once have been a 'bleak heath' but now it is grass. In 1381 Wat Tyler rallied the Peasants' Revolt here. Royal visitors include Henry V who arrived in triumph from the Battle of Agincourt and Henry VIII who greeted his new wife Anne of Cleves here, although she turned out to be less attractive than her portrait. The Princess of Wales pub is named after the Prince Regent's estranged wife Caroline, who lived in Greenwich Park. Blackheath Rugby Football Club, the world's oldest Rugby Union Football Club, was founded here at the pub in 1858.

12 *Wimbledon Common*

START	Tibbet's Corner
DISTANCE	3½ miles (5.6km)
TIME	2 hours
PARKING	Roadside parking in Wildcroft Road
ROUTE FEATURES	Woodland and paths which can be muddy

Putney Heath and adjacent Wimbledon Common together form over a thousand acres of woods, heath, ponds and streams. Although divided by the now busy Portsmouth road they are both cleverly linked by tunnels which allow for long walks or horse rides. There are plenty of rabbits and more dragonflies than anywhere else in London.

Putney Heath, which sees an occasional deer and has a cattle pound, is alongside the Portsmouth road. Highwayman Dick Turpin is said to have hidden his pistols at the Green Man. A later daily drinker was poet Algernon Swinburn. Another pub, the Telegraph, recalls the Admiralty telegraph erected here in 1796 as part of a link to Portsmouth and operated with shutters. Constable paused to sketch the structure in 1812.

On leaving the bus terminus face the Green Man and turn left to walk along Wildcroft Road. At a crossroads go left to pass the Telegraph pub. Continue across a car park and along a path shared with a cycle lane.

At the corner go left with the main path. Walk down the subway which has lanes for cycles, horses and pedestrians. Stay on this path as it passes under and over roads at the Tibbet's Corner traffic junction.

A On the far side the hard path gives way to gravel. Ignore all turnings as the path bends to the south. Soon, at a junction, there is a glimpse to the right of Kings Mere pond. There is a parallel path to the right as the way, known as the Ladies Mile, runs across heath. Later, on emerging from trees, there is a sudden view of the windmill above a cluster of low buildings.

PUBLIC TRANSPORT Bus from Putney Station to the Green Man pub
REFRESHMENTS Windmill Tearoom
PUBLIC TOILETS Alongside windmill
ORDNANCE SURVEY MAPS OS Explorer 161 (London South)

B Go to the right round the buildings passing the tearoom and the London Scottish Golf Club entrance. Turn left along a third side and at the end, before a fourth side, go sharp right down a straight woodland path. At the bottom keep to the right of Queen's Mere pond. At the far end continue ahead through trees to a T-junction opposite a closed cemetery gate.

C Turn right along Stag Ride. At a five-way junction bear half left on the wide path which runs steeply up Jerry's Hill. Later there is Jerry's Pond to the left. Stay by the

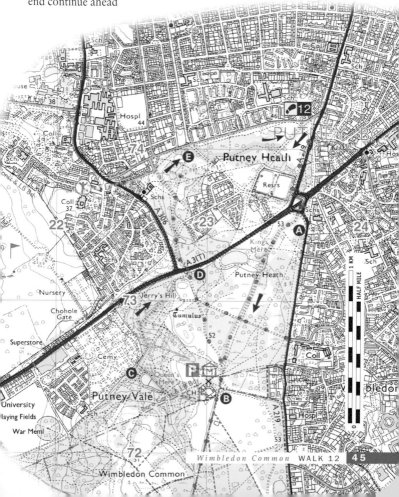

Queen's Mere

water to continue forward to meet a path running under a road.

D Go through the tunnel. On the far side is Putney Common with a

> The windmill, built in 1817, is the only remaining example of a hollow-post flour mill. Nearby **Queen's Mere** pond was dug in 1887 to mark Queen Victoria's Golden Jubilee. William Pitt survived a dual on the common the year before he introduced income tax as a temporary measure.

brief view of Roehampton Lane to the left before the path runs downhill through trees and past Scio Pond. At the fork take the left hand path. Follow the main track which soon passes a hollow known as the Frying Pan. To the left there is a view of Holy Trinity, Roehampton's 200-foot spire. Just past the war memorial and before a road go right on a gravel path. This briefly runs hard by the road.

E Here go right into Telegraph Road. Walk as far as Cross Roads Cottage on the left. Go through the gateway at the side and at the back bear right. Stay on this woodland path across all junctions. There is a cricket field in the trees to the right. At Wildcroft Road turn left for the Green Man and the bus terminus. ●

? *Why do Scouts visit the windmill?*

Nonsuch

START Cheam
DISTANCE 4 miles (7km)
TIME 3 hours
PARKING Kingsway Road car park (pay and display)
ROUTE FEATURES Park and woodland paths

In Philip of Spain's Escorial Palace there is a map of England which includes Nonsuch Palace. Now it cannot be found on any modern map. The site of the lost palace remains a vast grass space midway between London's border villages of Cheam and Ewell. The park is full of interest and sometimes woodpeckers can be heard.

Leave Cheam Station by the 'London' platform on the north side. Turn right out of the station approach and walk along Station Way to a crossroads by the High Street. Cross over and turn left along Ewell Road which runs past shops and then the side of Cheam Park.

A Where the road bends keep ahead through the gates of Nonsuch Park on the London boundary. Soon the pavement ends but beyond a gate the path is traffic free. After some distance the leafy way passes a modern house called Castlemain Lodge by a junction.

B At Castlemain Lodge only turn right to see three stones marking the site of Nonsuch Palace. The third stone has a plan of the house and its two courtyards. The main walk continues ahead up the slope. At the divide take the right hand

Nonsuch Palace was built in 1538 for Henry VIII who cleared a village to make space and brought stone from Merton Priory which he had just closed down. The name suggests that it was intended to be without compare and Italian craftsmen worked on the building. Charles II gave it to his mistress Barbara Villiers but she sold it to Lord Berkeley who had it demolished. Today's nearby Nonsuch House was built in 1804 to a design by Sir Jeffrey Wyatville who remodelled Windsor Castle.

PUBLIC TRANSPORT Rail to Cheam from Victoria Station
REFRESHMENTS Nonsuch House café
PUBLIC TOILETS Nonsuch House
ORDNANCE SURVEY MAPS OS Explorer 161 (London South)

At a post marked 5 turn right out of the trees into a field which has a raised area with low brick walls. This is the remains of a platform on which stood a timber framed banqueting house or hunting lodge. At the end of the field bear left along the north side and in the corner down steps to a dual carriageway. Cross the road with care and on the far side go slightly to the right to find steps and a path.

Bourne Hall gateway

path with the rough surface and waymarked London Loop. A woodland path runs ahead.

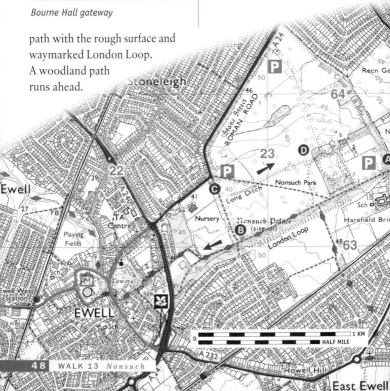

At the far end go ahead along Church Street. To the left is the Castle and on the right is the old 15th-century church tower standing alone. At a crossroads go right along the High Street and past the entrance to Bourne Hall.

Stay on the road as it passes the Spring Hotel and becomes London Road to pass today's Ewell Church. Keep to the right and cross the crossroads to continue ahead

> **Cheam Church** is known to Prince Philip who attended services here as a schoolboy at Cheam School. The Lumley Chapel outside, containing tombs of Nonsuch resident Lord Lumley and his two wives, is the chancel of the original medieval church. In the main road are the 18th-century Rectory, weatherboarded cottages and early 15th-century Whitehall all in a row.

between the purple Jim Thompson's building and the BP garage.

C Where the main road turns sharp left go right into Nonsuch Park using the kissing gate at the side. Bear half left to the side of the car park and go through the gate into the dog free field. Walk half right across the centre passing between two lonely trees.

Go through the gate in the corner and turn right for a few yards across the end of the Long Ditch. Turn left to walk westwards across the grass keeping a clump of trees over to the left

whilst heading for Nonsuch House in the distance.

D On the far side join a metalled path from the right which runs into the Nonsuch House grounds. Follow the path round the front of the house. After the double bend at the end at once go left past a car park on a path running into the woods. Ignore all turnings on the rising path to reach a gate (on the London boundary) leading into the grassed Cheam Recreation Ground.

Continue ahead and on the far side go to left round the children's playground to leave the ground at a gateway. Turn left past a car park and down the short residential Tudor Close. Turn right up Maldon Road to pass the church to the left and a series of historic houses on the right including Whitehall where a board indicates all the special houses.

Continue ahead to reach the starting point of the walk at Cheam Station.

> **?** *What is recorded on the milestone in the flowerbed near the Bourne Hall gateway?*

The Old Farmhouse at Cheam

Ashtead and Epsom

START Ashtead	**14**
DISTANCE 4½ miles (7.2km)	
TIME 3 hours	
PARKING Roadside parking next to station	
ROUTE FEATURES Woodland paths	

Epsom Common, adjacent to Epsom, merges with Ashtead Common to create a large nature reserve along the southern edge of London's boundary. Indeed the Ashtead half is appropriately managed by the Corporation of London whose coat of arms may surprise those alighting from the train at Ashtead Station, where the countryside runs right up to the level crossing.

From Ashtead Station walk on to the footpath opposite the level crossing by the Corporation of London sign. Walk ahead alongside Wood Field and over The Rye stream. Ahead are two main paths. Take the left hand ride (but not the sharp left path) with white arrow posts. The grass path gently climbs the hill and later enjoys various surfaces and widths as it bends across the wooded common. Ignore all turnings and eventually the way has a firm surface as it begins to run downhill to a Corporation of London sign and information board by New Pond.

Ashtead Common, a 500-acre ancient wooded common alongside open countryside, has been a national nature reserve since 1995. There are at least 2000 ancient oak pollards and rare wood pasture. Also recorded are 50 different tree species and shrubs and more than 300 plant species, including the greater yellow rattle, wood anemone and the southern marsh orchid. In early summer bluebells transform the ground. Deer can often be seen.

? *What are the white posts on the northern edge of Ashtead Common?*

A A path runs past stables to a road where, just beyond a bus stop to the right, there is the Star pub. The main walk continues to the

PUBLIC TRANSPORT Rail to Ashtead Station from Waterloo
REFRESHMENTS The Star pub in Kingston Road
PUBLIC TOILETS None
ORDNANCE SURVEY MAPS OS Explorer 161 (London South) and 146 (Dorking)

Woodland path on Ashtead Common

it passes a pond to the left. There are two signed footpaths to Rushett Lane crossing the way before the path crosses a wide path marking the boundary between Ashtead Common and Epsom Common.

Ⓑ Still keep ahead to pass Stew Pond to the right. The path is now near a road, and traffic can often be heard. Soon the Thames Down Link joins from the left having crossed the road. The trees thin out and after a short distance the path begins to gently bend to the right and has a grass surface.

Ⓒ At a junction with another wide grass ride (where there is a seat) go right and downhill to join a firm path swinging in from the left. Keep ahead at a T-junction to pass a sign indicating the boundary with Ashtead Common. On meeting the straight Ashtead–Epsom boundary path go left for a few yards and then right on to another straight path.

right passing the pond on the right. The firm path runs gently uphill following the Common boundary on the left which is also the London County boundary. The open countryside on the far side of the fence is within the London Borough of Kingston.

Later there is a signposted path to the left running across to Rushett Farm. A little further on a path runs off to the right through the trees to an earthwork. Stay on the main boundary path which rises as

D At the next junction keep ahead past the left turn but at the next left turn go left. Ahead can be seen a road but after only a few yards turn right on to a clear path free of horse riders. The path runs ahead rising slightly.

E At brushwood barriers cross a wide ride and look left to see a view of the Epsom Downs racecourse stand. Continue ahead and at the next wide ride go left and walk downhill. The spire of

> **Epsom Common** was owned by Chertsey Abbey, which dug the ponds to provide a fish supply. During a drought in 1618 a cowman discovered a spring which produced the original Epsom Salts. The Epsom Well attracted such people as Samuel Pepys and Daniel Defoe, but by 1740 interest had vanished, as other spas became more fashionable.

Headley Church (also a famous landmark from Epsom Downs racecourse) can be seen on the horizon. On reaching the stream go ahead to reach Ashtead Station. ●

15 *Farnborough*

START The George at Farnborough
DISTANCE 4½miles (7.2km)
TIME 3 hours
PARKING Limited roadside parking in Church Road and High Street
ROUTE FEATURES Field and woodland paths which may be muddy

This walk is through Kent countryside trapped inside the London borough of Bromley and across an 18th-century prime minister's estate. The Keston Ponds, source of the River Ravensbourne which runs into the Thames at Deptford, are found by the earthworks on Keston Common which has the remains of the oldest mill in Kent.

From the George walk down Church Road keeping on the right. The pavement continues as the raised approach to the lychgate at the churchyard. Walk past the church door and through the

The George and the **Change of Horses** are former coaching inns for the London-Hastings coach route. The church has a 14th-century font and a memorial to Thomas Young who translated the hieroglyphics on the Rosetta stone in the British Museum. Those who have worshipped here include prime minister William Gladstone, who came in 1876 when staying with Lord Avebury, the inventor of Bank Holidays, at nearby High Elms.

churchyard passing Gypsy Lee's grave on the right.

At the gate bear half right. The path is soon alongside a seat and trees. Where the path divides go left. The way is downhill to reach a kissing gate. Keep forward to another kissing gate by the road. Cross Shire Lane and go ahead up North End Lane. The road bends and rises to pass North End Farm.

Ⓐ Well before the cottages turn right into Bogey Lane. The stoney track rises. After a short distance go up steps on the left to follow a high parallel path in the field. Before the path swings left go right

PUBLIC TRANSPORT Bus from Bromley South Station
REFRESHMENTS Pubs in Farnborough
PUBLIC TOILETS Church Road in Farnborough and Keston Common
ORDNANCE SURVEY MAPS Explorer 147 (Sevenoaks & Tonbridge)

by posts down steps to return to the lane and take the right fork. Follow the path to the end to turn right down a road called Farthing Street. After a double bend the lane meets Shire Lane.

Cross over to find a path running to the left behind the hedge. Up to the right there is soon a clear view of Holwood mansion. Cross two stiles to follow a path round the back of a house.

B At the stile next stile do not go ahead to the road but turn sharp right to go round the barriers and follow an enclosed path uphill. In the wood at the top there are seats positioned on each side of a fence marking the site of the Wilberforce Oak. The path continues in an almost straight line onto Westerham Road. Cross over the road on to Keston Common and turn right to walk along a sunken path in the earthworks.

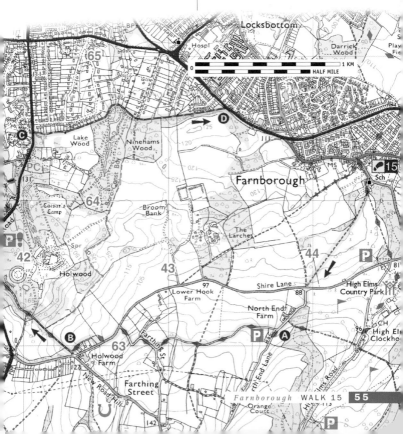

The **Wilberforce Oak** is in the grounds of Holwood, which was the home of William Pitt the Younger who became Prime Minister in 1783 at the age of 25. The stone seat marks the spot where in 1788 William Wilberforce told Pitt that he intended to abolish slavery. Today's oak is grown from an acorn taken from the historic oak.

At the far end cross a car park and go down steps to the River Ravensbourne source. Keep to the right of the pond ahead. Before the second pond bear right. Do not be tempted back to the pond but at another divide keep left to reach the end of Fishponds Road.

C Go left past the bus stop to walk along the main road passing the entrance to Holwood. Just before the first house on the right turn right to follow a footpath. This fenced wooded bridlepath runs for a mile along the north side of the Holwood estate.

D At a main road turn right and at a junction go right again into Farnborough High Street to reach the George.

What is unusual about the milestone, almost opposite the Change of Horses, in Farnborough High Street?

The Wilberforce seat

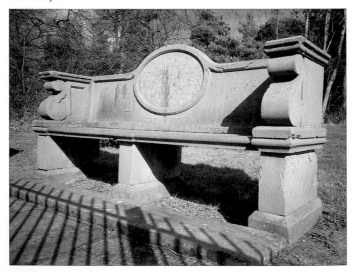

Merstham

16

START Merstham
DISTANCE 4½ miles (7.2km)
TIME 3 hours
PARKING Roadside parking near station
ROUTE FEATURES Parkland and steep woodland path

Merstham, a village on the London to Brighton road, has a beautiful street named after a West End stage success. Nearby Gatton, on the ancient Pilgrims' Way, has the country's smallest town hall in a 'Capability' Brown landscape. Looking down on this Home Counties countryside is Nut Wood, where you can find orchids, butterflies and viewpoints.

From Merstham Station bear half right to walk up Station Road. Cross the main road to walk down Old Mill Lane at the side of the Railway Arms and reach Quality Street. Turn left and go right at the entrance to the cricket club. The path is waymarked North Downs

Quality Street

PUBLIC TRANSPORT Rail to Merstham Station, London Bridge or Victoria Station
REFRESHMENTS Railway Arms in Merstham
PUBLIC TOILETS None
ORDNANCE SURVEY MAPS OS Explorer 146 (Dorking)

Merstham's **Quality Street**, once the main road to Brighton, is named after the play by JM Barrie. Major Quality and Miss Sweetly were played by Seymour Hicks and Ellaline Terriss who lived at the 15th-century Old Forge at the north-east end. The launch of the famous sweets in 1936 coincided with the film version and it is suggested that the street scene on the round tin was inspired by this street and village where there are bow-fronted houses. Quality Street has been compared to the film set village of Denham on the edge of north London. The Pilgrims' Way probably ran through the churchyard of the partly 13th-century St Katherine's. Now it is stranded above the motorway and reached by a footpath at the end of Quality Street, which is the old main road, and a bridge.

Way, the national trail name for the Pilgrims' Way. A path runs downhill and along the side of the cricket field to a kissing gate.

Follow the path ahead which runs uphill over a golf course. Soon after crossing an estate road leave the path by going through a kissing gate on to a parallel path sheltered from the motorway noise. Later the path reaches a group of houses. At a road go left and then right to walk towards the Gatton Park gateway.

Go through the gate next to the thatched lodge and follow the drive to a junction. To the left is a short road leading to Gatton Church. Ahead is a gateway to a private school drive where the pillars of the open-sided 'town hall' are just visible. To the right is a modern school chapel.

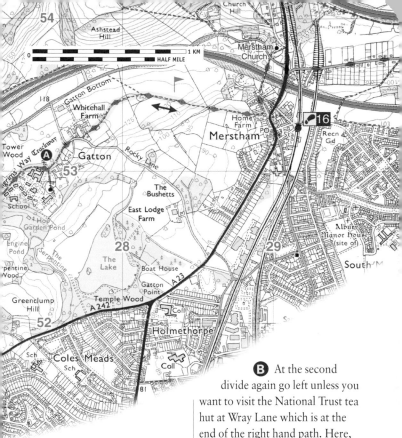

A Turn right past the chapel and follow the estate road round the corner past new buildings and downhill. Continue ahead uphill past the 'no exit' sign. Beyond a gate the way is wooded.

Just before a building on the left turn left by a National Trust sign on to a path running up into Great Buck Wood. At the first divide keep left.

B At the second divide again go left unless you want to visit the National Trust tea hut at Wray Lane which is at the end of the right hand path. Here, at this North Downs Way refreshment stop, there is a panoramic view which includes Gatwick airport.

The main walk continues to the left of the divide downhill past a break in the trees affording a view over Gatton. Turn left with the main path which runs down and uphill through a gateway. At the top the wide woodland path soon bears

Bluebells in Nut Wood

left and later right before running steeply downhill.

C At the bottom go left. This path, on a high shelf, runs gently down to join a path from the right.

Gatton, which takes its name from a gate on the Winchester to Canterbury Pilgrims' Way, was a rotten borough having received the status from Henry VI who wanted support for his marriage to Margaret of Anjou. Although there were never more than 23 people here, the 'town' elected two Members of Parliament until 1832. There is even a tiny Town Hall built for the declaration of the poll. Gatton Hall, now a school, was in the 20th century the seat of Sir Jeremiah Colman.

The way is between fields with a view down on to The Lake. At the top of a slope the path meets a junction of metalled estate roads.

D Go ahead uphill to begin retracing the outward route. Follow the road to pass the thatched lodge and at the Bulb Nursery sign go left to pass the Dower House. The path leads back to the cricket ground. At Merstham's Quality Street go left and right into Old Mill Lane to the Railway Arms public house. Continue over the main road and ahead to reach Merstham Station and the starting point of the walk. ●

Addington

START Coombe Lane	
DISTANCE 4½ miles (7.2km)	
TIME 3 hours	
PARKING None (parking in Croydon)	
ROUTE FEATURES Grass and woodland paths	

Part of the fun in visiting Addington is arriving by tram which runs out of Croydon and travels fast on its own track up through the woods of Addington Hills before plunging down Gravel Hill to the attractive village. This recent transport improvement makes Croydon's surprise countryside and viewpoint easily accessible.

Follow the path from the Coombe Lane Tram Stop through the trees with Coombe Lane over to the right. Later the path joins the road. Use the crossing at the main junction ahead to cross over to the gateway next to Ballards Lane on the right.

Go through the gateway into Heathfield Gardens. At once go left by the lodge and follow the straight path through the bushes and down steps to a road by a pond. Turn right to go across the back of the pond and up steps. At the top go right up more steps. Cross a car park and go left down Riesco Drive.

Where the houses end keep ahead into the London Wildlife Trust's wood. Follow the path past the viewpoint and through the rest of

Addington village has a remarkable church and a working forge which is at least 250 years old. Nearby Addington Palace was in the 19th century the Archbishop of Canterbury's country home, which is why a cross in the churchyard records the names of five Archbishops buried in the church. The reredos inside was added in 1896 as a memorial to Archbishop Benson who was the last to live here and introduced at this church the now traditional Nine Lessons and Carols service at Christmas. The Palace's Lion Lodges on Spout Hill date from the 1770s.

PUBLIC TRANSPORT Tramlink from East Croydon Station to Coombe Lane
REFRESHMENTS Addington Village Inn at Addington
PUBLIC TOILETS Addington Hills
ORDNANCE SURVEY MAPS OS Explorer 161 (London South)

wooded Bramley Bank Nature Reserve. At the far end go through the kissing gate.

A Bear left across the grass to follow a road called Broadcoombe downhill past St Francis Church.

Soon after the houses on the left end, affording a view, go ahead along a passage as the road swings away. At the end by Gilbert Scott School turn left to follow a wide path downhill to reach Gravel Hill Tram Stop.

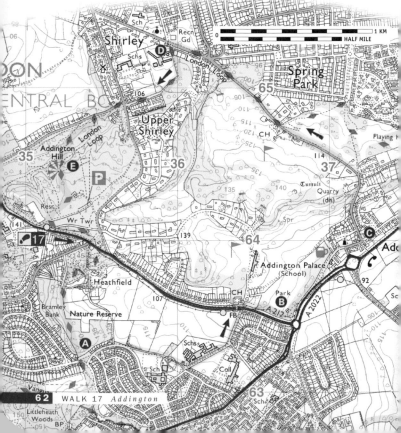

Cross the track and the bridge over the road. Turn right to walk past the Addington Palace lodge with the tram tracks down to the right.

B After a short distance go left through a gate and along a short path into a large meadow. Bear right round the field (or across the centre if there are no games or visiting fun fair) to reach a gate in the bottom corner. Turn left to walk through Addington passing the pub and the church.

C Go left up Spout Hill. After Addington Palace's Lion Gate the pavement is briefly above the road. At the top stay on this road as it runs past Kennel Wood, Shirley Heath and later Foxes Wood. After a small roundabout there is a view across a recreation ground to the right.

D Turn left into Pinewoods. Follow the path round on the edge of the wood and round two sides of a playing field. Walk ahead down residential Sandpits Road. At the main Shirley Road cross over to walk down Oaks Road opposite.

Keep on left side and after a short distance go through a gate on the left. A path runs through the trees to a junction. Turn right and follow a path, waymarked with London Loop discs on posts, which rises.

E At the top there is a clearing with a viewpoint platform ahead. From the platform turn round and follow the flat gravel path. At a house (a restaurant but not a café) turn right. A path runs into the trees. Keep left at a divide and right at a T-junction. Just before the path runs steeply downhill go left on a narrow path to reach Coombe Lane Tram Stop. ●

View from Addington Hills

● Ancient churches ● woodland ● pretty valley

18 *Coulsdon*

START Old Coulsdon
DISTANCE 5 miles (8km)
TIME 3 hours
PARKING Car park behind the Fox pub on Coulsdon Common
ROUTE FEATURES Grassy valley and church with wall painting

Hilltop Old Coulsdon and nearby Chaldon, just a few yards outside London's boundary, both have remarkable churches. The rural nature of the area in between has been preserved largely thanks to the Corporation of London which in the 19th century stepped in to halt the threatened spread of suburbia into this outstanding countryside.

Old Coulsdon has a green complete with a pond and a Tudor-style shopping parade. The church, with its 15th-century tower, was built in 1260 but was dramatically enlarged in 1959 when a new nave was added on the south side turning the original church into a chapel. Next to the old high altar there is a rare 13th-century sedilia and piscina–seats for clergy and a basin.

Start at the war memorial on the corner of Canon's Hill opposite the shops. Walk along the road towards the church. But before the church lychgate turn right down the side of The Corner Cottage. A path runs along the side of the churchyard and along the bottom of several gardens. Where the way turns sharply right keep ahead downhill on the rough path.

At a residential road go left down to a junction and turn right into Caterham Drive. Beyond a bus stop and opposite Keston Avenue turn left on to a footpath. The way rises steeply up a wooded hillside to a track.

A Go right on the track and after a house keep ahead on a footpath running through a wood. The path on the ground tends to weave

? *In the wall painting who are the people on the bridge of spikes in the right hand corner?*

PUBLIC TRANSPORT Bus from Coulsdon Station
REFRESHMENTS Pubs in Coulsdon and on Coulsdon Common
PUBLIC TOILETS None
ORDNANCE SURVEY MAPS OS Explorer 146 (Dorking)

COULSDON

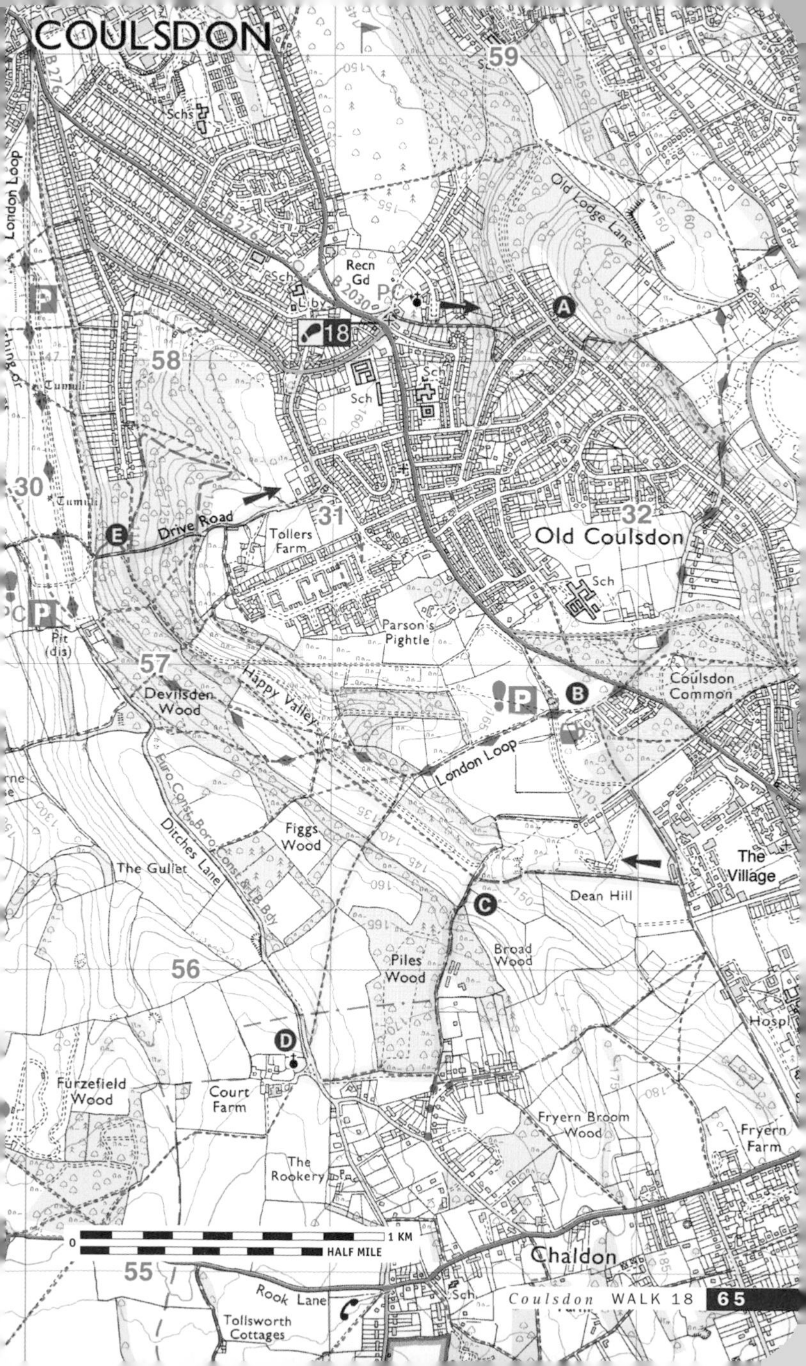

B 276
Schs
59
Old Lodge Lane
London Loop
Recn Gd
Sch
Liby
B 2030
PC
18
A
58
Sch
Tumuli
Tumulus
30
E
Drive Road
31
Tollers Farm
32
Old Coulsdon
Sch
PC
P
Pit (dis)
Parson's Pightle
57
Devilsden Wood
Happy Valley
B
Coulsdon Common
London Loop
Euro Const Boro Const & LB Bdy
Ditches Lane
Figgs Wood
The Gullet
The Village
C
Dean Hill
Broad Wood
Piles Wood
56
D
Hospl
Furzefield Wood
Court Farm
Fryern Broom Wood
Fryern Farm
The Rookery
0
1 KM
HALF MILE
Chaldon
55
Rook Lane
Sch
Tollsworth Cottages

Tiny **Chaldon Church** is listed in the 1086 Domesday Book and has a remarkable wall painting which was added about a century later. The artist was probably a monk. This teaching aid which predates printing was whitewashed over sometime in the Tudor period but discovered by accident in 1869 when decorators were cleaning the west wall. The picture, one of Europe's finest church wall paintings, depicts the Ladder of Salvation with Hell below and Heaven above.

round fallen trees. At the far end go right again downhill through the trees on a steep path running down to a road.

Go ahead up Rydon's Lane which narrows as it climbs up on to Coulsdon Common. At a T-junction cross the road and go ahead on a woodland path with cottages in a clearing over to the left. Cross Coulsdon Road to go ahead up Fox Lane.

B Turn left across the front of the Fox pub and walk over grass to a gate on the far side. Continue forward through thin woodland to another gate. Continue over a lane and directly ahead. To the left is The Village, a new development on the site of Caterham Barracks. Much of the military brick wall on the left remains by the path. At a junction, by a house balcony, go right on to a bridleway. Soon the way runs gently downhill into green Happy Valley.

C Here turn left to take a woodland path running uphill.

Path from Chaldon Church

Lychgate and stone stile at Old Coulsdon

Later there are houses to the left. On approaching a green turn right on a path signposted ' Chaldon Church'. The way is between the wood and a field. At the bottom the land drops down to a road. Go right and almost at once left up to Chaldon Church.

D On leaving the church turn left at the divide and go left again for a few yards. Bear right where a signpost points to 'Happy Valley'. A footpath runs over the hill and down through a strip of woodland to the top of the valley. Go downhill to bear left along the valley floor.

After running through trees, the wide open way narrows and then a horse ride sweeps in from the right. Eventually the path further narrows to a six-way junction.

E Turn right up the path signposted 'Bridleway 742'. The woodland path runs steeply up the side of the valley. Keep forward to pass stables at Tollers Lodge and then Tollers Farm. Where the lane divides behind Tollers Cottage keep left to a junction.

Turn left along residential Tollers Lane. (The bus stop is served by buses to Coulsdon South Station.) At a crossroads by grass go right along Placehouse Lane to pass Coulsdon College and reach the shops in the centre of Old Coulsdon.

●

19 *Petts Wood*

START Petts Wood
DISTANCE 5 ½ miles (8.9km)
TIME 3 ½ hours
PARKING Jubilee Park
ROUTE FEATURES Woodland paths which can be muddy

Chislehurst was part of Kent until 1965 and, thanks to the National Trust, still has a rural feel. Here there is farmland with sheep, cattle and horses. A park has a nature reserve and a ruined moated manor house. A royal tomb is one of several historic memorials in the two attractive churches on Chislehurst Common.

Leave Petts Wood Station by turning left on reaching the bridge from the platform. Go down the steps and ahead to go right along Queensway. Continue into Crest View Drive and go right into Tent Peg Lane. Take the concrete path by the car park but soon turn on to the parallel woodland path to avoid the cycle lane.

At a junction go right down an enclosed path which suddenly bends to the foot of a bridge spanning Petts Wood Junction. At the end a woodland path turns away from the railway to follow a line of gardens. The way crosses a road and two further railway bridges.

Chislehurst Common's **St Nicholas Church** has the tomb of Sir Edmund Walsingham who lived at the now abandoned moated manor in Scadbury Park. St Mary's has a mausoleum attached built for the body of Napoleon III who died at nearby Camden Place. He is now interred at Farnborough Abbey but the body of the Prince Imperial who died in the Zulu War remains.

A Follow the path ahead with the railway to the left and fields to the right. The path turns north on to National Trust land to run between open fields, across the Kyd Brook stream and uphill. On the left is Hawkwood's farmhouse with its Gothic-style windows. Continue up the track (from here called

PUBLIC TRANSPORT Rail to Petts Wood Station from Charing Cross or Victoria Station
REFRESHMENTS Pubs in Chislehurst
PUBLIC TOILETS None
ORDNANCE SURVEY MAPS OS Explorer 162 (Greenwich)

Botany Bay Lane) which at a double bend enters Chislehurst with a metalled surface. Pass St Mary's on the corner of Crown Lane to reach the main road.

Cross over and go through the lychgate and through the churchyard passing the ancient St Nicholas Church to the left. At Church Lane turn left to reach the crossroads by the Bull's Head in the village's shopping centre.

? *Why is there a large dip in the grass on Chislehurst Common between the parish church and the Crown pub?*

B Continue directly ahead down Bull Lane. On the way there is Easdens to the right. Just beyond the right hand turning is Murrabinda, Ted Willis's home, marked with a plaque. Continue forward to pass a green and join a main road where there is an entrance to Farringtons School.

Hawkwood Farm

C Go right into Old Perry Street. Just before the Sidney Arms go right into Scadbury Park. Beyond the car park bear left on a woodland path. Shortly after a picnic area the path bends to meet a metalled roadway leading to Scadbury Park Farm on the right. Cross over to go through the kissing gate and turn sharp right. Soon there is another kissing gate behind a house. Follow the

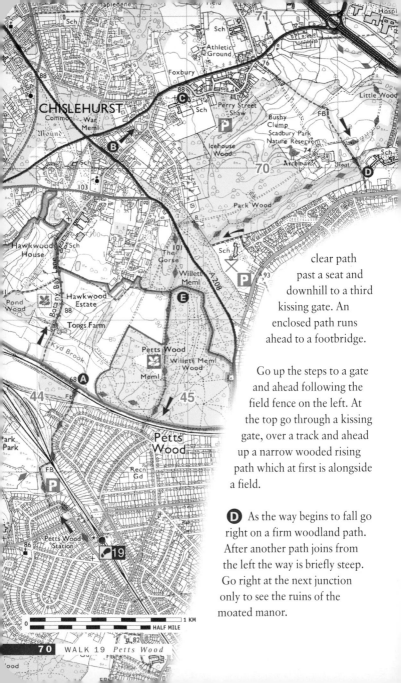

clear path past a seat and downhill to a third kissing gate. An enclosed path runs ahead to a footbridge.

Go up the steps to a gate and ahead following the field fence on the left. At the top go through a kissing gate, over a track and ahead up a narrow wooded rising path which at first is alongside a field.

D As the way begins to fall go right on a firm woodland path. After another path joins from the left the way is briefly steep. Go right at the next junction only to see the ruins of the moated manor.

The main walk continues ahead. Later the way passes under a giant oak. Keep forward past a seat at a four way junction and at the next junction keep a seat to the left but at a third seat turn left past a post. At a T-junction go right and then left on a metalled drive to reach a main road.

Cross over with care to take the path opposite by the gate on the edge of Petts Wood. At the divide keep left. Ignore all turnings to reach an enclosed triangle of grass with three exits.

Willett Memorial in Petts Wood

E To see the Willett Memorial go sharp left just before this junction. To continue the main

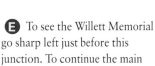
Petts Wood has ancient woodland and plants such as lily-of-the-valley. The trees include ancient oaks, birch, rowan, alder, ash, hornbeam and sweet chestnut. The wood takes it name from shipbuilder William Pett, who leased it for timber. It was bought by public subscription in 1927 as a memorial to William Willett, who had the idea of British Summer Time whilst riding here. The houses to the south were built after the railway station opened in 1928.

walk bear left in the triangle to pass a National Trust sign. The path runs along the edge of Petts Wood with fields to the right. Deeper in the wood there is a path junction with the Edlmann memorial over to the right. Keep forward and soon the path merges with another on the way to a tunnel under the railway.

At a road go left and then right into Towncourt Crescent. Beyond a crossroads go right by the Daylight Inn into Station Square to find Petts Wood Station. ●

● Views ● deer ● heathland ● riverside path

20 *Richmond*

START Richmond
DISTANCE 5½miles (8.9km)
TIME 3 hours
PARKING NCP car park next to station
ROUTE FEATURES Heathland paths

Richmond was a staging post on the Thames with its own Royal residence. Today its busy riverside remains attractive with water meadows close to the town centre.
Richmond Park is London's largest park with a varied landscape from gardens and plantations to heathland. The unfenced roads with wandering deer could be mistaken for a corner of Scotland.

At Richmond Station turn left to walk along The Quadrant and follow this main shopping street as it becomes George Street. Turn left into Hill Street and then go right down to Richmond Bridge where steps on either side of the bridge go down to the Thames towpath. Turn left upstream with the water to the right. Stay on the towpath even when it moves away from the riverside. Where it begins to turn back to the river go ahead through a kissing gate to follow the path across Petersham Meadows.

A On the far side keep forward round the barriers to pass Petersham church.

Petersham still has cows grazing on its meadows, which are rented out by the council at a peppercorn rent to preserve the timeless scene. Once Express Dairies owned nearby River Lane Farm to supply bottled milk to south-west London doorsteps. The partly Norman church has Georgian box pews making it impossible for all the congregation to see the altar. It is popular for weddings and those married here include the late Queen Mother's parents in 1881. Her sister, Violet Hyacinth, who died before the future Queen's birth, is buried in nearby Ham churchyard.

At the main road turn left. After Café Dysart go through an easily missed gate on the right at the end

PUBLIC TRANSPORT Underground (District Line) or rail (from Waterloo) to Richmond Station
REFRESHMENTS Pembroke Lodge café in Richmond Park
PUBLIC TOILETS Pembroke Lodge
ORDNANCE SURVEY MAPS Explorer 161 (London South)

of the railings just before the bus stop. Bear half left uphill where a signpost points to Pembroke Lodge. When the path appears to divide keep to the left to continue uphill to a small gate. Go left up to a path in the grounds of Pembroke Lodge.

To see the view from the top of Henry VIII's Mound go left and take the second right just before the tunnel. The main walk continues to the right. Follow the path ahead along the edge of the garden to pass across the back of Pembroke Lodge. At the far end of the garden go through a gate.

B Continue forward on the path over to the left. This winds ahead between the firm cycling track by

Keyhole view of Richmond Park

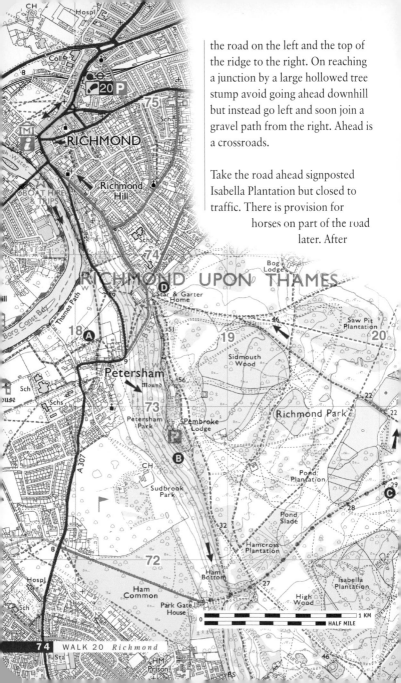

the road on the left and the top of
the ridge to the right. On reaching
a junction by a large hollowed tree
stump avoid going ahead downhill
but instead go left and soon join a
gravel path from the right. Ahead is
a crossroads.

Take the road ahead signposted
Isabella Plantation but closed to
traffic. There is provision for
horses on part of the road
later. After

passing the dense trees of Pond Plantation to the left look out for the road widening by a seat. There is a glimpse of water to the left.

C Turn left on a path by the seat. It soon curves to cross a cutting. Ignore a left turn and follow the path to join a wide path which runs between the two Penn Ponds. Keep ahead uphill to pass alongside the enclosed Sidmouth Wood to the

> **?** *The church notice board at Petersham mentions Vancouver's grave. Why is George Vancouver famous?*

The Vineyard, off Richmond Hill

James I enclosed Shene Chase to create **Richmond Park** where at least 600 red and fallow deer wander. Around 100 are culled each year under the Royal Venison Warrant which allows such figures as the Archbishop of Canterbury to receive a quarter of venison at Christmas. The Lord Mayor of London, who entertains with banquets, can claim four quarters. Queen Mary spent part of her childhood at White Lodge where her son Edward VIII was born. Today Thatched House Lodge is the home of Princess Alexandra. Pembroke Lodge, now a café, was the home of Lord John Russell, one of Queen Victoria's early Prime Ministers. His grandson philosopher Bertrand Russell spent part of his childhood here. In the garden there is the remarkable keyhole view from the top of Henry VIII's Mound giving a direct view of St Paul's Cathedral 10 miles (16km) away.

left. To the right there is a view of the BT Tower and the City. Do not curve left with the path and wood but keep going forward to join the road on the right. Follow the grass path at the roadside to the park gates.

D Walk pass the Star & Garter Home to follow the road ahead past a viewpoint and downhill into Richmond. Retrace your steps from here back to Richmond Station. ●

Further Information

Walking Safety

Although the countryside within the M25 and Greater London has few dangers care should still be taken. Some country paths, even in a London Borough, can be a distance from a road or house so Country Code rules should still be applied.

Paths can unexpectedly be wet and slippery and sensible shoes should always be worn. Comfortable shoes are just as important in the city where there are many more metalled paths. However, managed woodland and forest bridlepaths often have carefully laid surfaces which withstand both rain and horses hooves.

Care should be taken when near rivers or streams. The Thames and River Lea can be dangerous if not treated with respect and walkers should always remain on the towpath or riverside path and not enter the water, however tempting on a hot day.

In warm weather, it is advisable to carry a drink and not rely on the pub always being open in the afternoon. Water is always best on a walk rather than a fizzy or orange drink. A plastic bottle almost filled with water and kept in the freezer overnight will melt slowly when carried in a rucksack on a hot day and provide a welcome cold drink before reaching a café or home.

Care is also needed when crossing the capital's very busy roads and in the city centre the visitor should be aware of possible traffic when stopping to look at a view or historic building. Where there is no pavement you should always walk on the right hand side of the road to face on-coming traffic.

Follow the Country Code

- Enjoy the countryside and respect its life and work
- Guard against all risk of fire
- Take your litter home
- Fasten all gates
- Help to keep all water clean
- Keep your dogs under control
- Protect wildlife, plants and trees
- Keep to public paths across farmland
- Take special care on country roads
- Leave livestock, crops and machinery alone
- Make no unnecessary noise

Greenwich Park

- Use gates and stiles to cross
  fences, hedges and walls
                (The Countryside Agency)

Useful Organisations
Countryside Agency
South East & London Region:
Dacre House,19 Dacre Street,
London SW1H 0DH.
Tel. 020 7340 2900
Fax 020 7340 2999

Web-site: www.countryside.gov.uk

English Heritage
23 Savile Row, London W1X 1AB.
Tel. 020 7973 3434
Fax 020 7973 3001
Web site: www.english-
heritage.org.uk

Epping Forest
Information Centre, High Beach,

Loughton, IG10 4AF.
Tel.020 8508 0028
Fax 020 8532 0188
Web-site.
www.cityoflondon.gov.uk

Corporation of London
Guildhall, London EC2P 2EJ
Tel. 020 73323099
E-mail: pro@corpoflondon.gov.uk

Ashtead Common
Woodfield Road, Ashtead
KT21 2DU
Tel. 01372 279083
Fax 01372 271670

Web site:
www.cityoflondon.gov.uk/Ashtead

National Trust
Membership and general enquiries:
PO Box 39, Bromley,
Kent BR1 3XL
Tel. 0202 8315 1111
E-mail: enquiries@ntrust.org.uk

London Regional Office:
Hughenden Manor, High
Wycombe,
Buckinghamshire HP14 4LA
Tel. 01494 528051
Web site:
www.nationaltrust.org.uk

HMS Belfast

Ordnance Survey
Romsey Road, Maybush,
Southampton SO16 4GU.
Tel. 08456 05 05 05 (Lo-call)

Public transport
London Buses: 020 7222 1234
Railtrack: 08457 484950
Tramlink: 020 7222 1234
Underground: 020 7222 1234

Ramblers' Assocation
2nd Floor, Camelford House,
87-90 Albert Embankment
London SE1 7TW.
Tel. 020 7339 8500
Fax 020 7339 8501
Web-site: www.ramblers.org.uk

London Tourist Board
Written enquiries only to
Glen House, Stag Place,
London SW1E 5LT
E-mail: enquiries@
londontouristboard.co.uk
Web site:
www.londontouristboard.co.uk

Local tourist information centres:
Bromley: 020 8460 9955
Croydon: 020 8253 1009
Greenwich: 0870 608 2000
Richmond: 020 8940 9125
Southwark: 020 7403 8299

London Wildlife Trust
Harling House, 47-51 Great
Suffolk Street,
London SE1 0BS.
Tel. 020 7261 0447
Fax 020 7261 0538
E-mail: londonwt@cix.co.uk
Web-site: www.wildlondon.org.uk

Youth Hostels Association
Trevelyan House,
Dimple Road, Matlock,
Derbyshire DE4 3YH.
Tel. 01629 592600
Web site: www.yha.org.uk

*Ordnance Survey Maps of
South London*
Explorer maps 146 (Dorking), 147
(Sevenoaks), 161 (London South),
162 (Greenwich) and 173 (London
North).

Answers to Questions
Walk 1: A cat. It is part of a
sculpture with Dr Alfred Salter
sitting on a nearby seat waving at
his daughter.
Walk 2: Guy the Gorilla by David
Wynne 1962.
Walk 3: Elizabeth I who attended a
christening in the next door church.
Walk 4: They are boundary
markers denoting the old parish of
Camberwell Borough which was
absorbed into the London Borough
of Southwark. This is still the
boundary between the Boroughs of
Southwark and Lewisham.

Walk 5: A brick ice house built about 1760. Ice from the pond was stored there.

Walk 6: Croydon and Wandsworth.

Walk 7: The original railway bridge, carrying continental trains, rested on them from 1862 to 1985.

Walk 8: A mounting block for horse riders leaving the original pub which was opposite the steps.

Walk 9: An early 18th-century dovecot.

Walk 10: A lighthouse built for training lighthouse keepers.

Walk 11: Prince Phillip or The Duke of Edinburgh.

Walk 12: A plaque records that Lord Baden-Powell wrote Scouting for Boys here five years before the first Scout Camp in 1907.

Walk 13: London is 14 miles away. The measurement is taken from Trafalgar Square.

Walk 14: Coal tax posts. The Corporation of London had the right to levy tax on coal crossing a wide boundary around London. The money was used to help rebuild St Paul's Cathedral after the Great Fire. These posts date from 1861.

Walk 15: Sevenoaks is spelt Seven Oaks.

Walk 16: Colman's Mustard.

Walk 17: To mark Croydon's own Millenary year.

Walk 18: Dishonest traders. The person on the left is a milkman who gave short measure and now has to carry a brimming container.

Walk 19: It is a former cock pit. People took bets on fighting cocks before the sport was declared cruel and illegal in 1834.

Walk 20: He gave his name to Vancouver in Canada.